CIRCUS OF FEARS

ROAR!

Haunting HUMAN PHOBIAS

by John Wood &
Noah Leatherland

BEARPORT
PUBLISHING

Minneapolis, Minnesota

Credits
Images are courtesy of Shutterstock.com. With thanks to Getty Images, Thinkstock Photo, and iStockphoto. RECURRING – Denys Koltovskyi, vectorlight, v_v_v, pikepicture. COVER – Vladimir Gjorgiev, vectorlight, Denys Koltovskyi, ONYXprj, Ground Picture, Tartila, v_v_v. 4–5 – The Faces, sicegame. 6–7 – Evgeniya Litovchenko, VectorPunks, Hohum. 8–9 – Enrique Romero, Sarah Guilford. 10–11 – andriano.cz, Nick Hawkes. 12–13 – sciencepics, Kateryna Kon. 14–15 – icon0.com, lingdamphotothailand, karelnoppe, iconriver, Gavrilo Stanojevic. 16–17 – Alex Mit, klyots, Anastasi17. 18–19 – Shuravaya, viviana loza, GoodStudio. 20–21 – Terdsak L, LightField Studios, C Design Studio. 22–23 – Lemonreader, 995577823Xyn (WikiCommons). 24–25 – Pavel Krasensky, Prostock-studio, WinWin artlab. 26–27 – Lisa F. Young, nito. 28–29 – Torychemistry, UfaBizPhoto, YummyBuum. 30–31 – pikepicture.

Bearport Publishing Company Product Development Team
President: Jen Jenson; Director of Product Development: Spencer Brinker; Managing Editor: Allison Juda; Associate Editor: Naomi Reich; Associate Editor: Tiana Tran; Art Director: Colin O'Dea; Designer: Elena Klinkner; Designer: Kayla Eggert; Product Development Assistant: Owen Hamlin

Library of Congress Cataloging-in-Publication Data is available at www.loc.gov or upon request from the publisher.

ISBN: 979-8-88916-609-2 (hardcover)
ISBN: 979-8-88916-614-6 (paperback)
ISBN: 979-8-88916-618-4 (ebook)

For more information, write to Bearport Publishing, 5357 Penn Avenue South, Minneapolis, MN 55419.

CONTENTS

WELCOME

★ TO THE ★

SHOW!

COME ONE, COME ALL! SEE THE AMAZING CIRCUS OF FEARS!

Everyone is afraid of something. But do you have a phobia? This is a very strong fear. You may even have a phobia of something that cannot cause you any real danger.

People have phobias of all sorts of things. Some common phobias are of spiders or flying on planes.

Our circus is all about real fears. Are you ready to find out what scares people the most?

Maybe you will leave with a brand-new phobia of your own. . . .

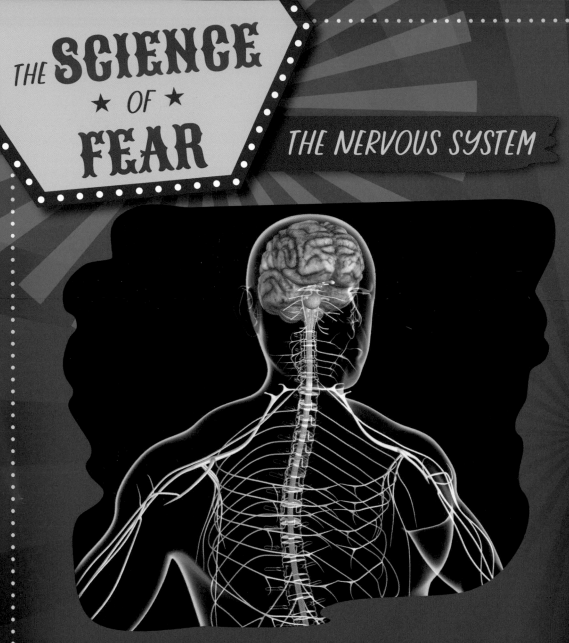

Your nervous system is the network of **nerves** that send messages throughout your body. You can control some messages, such as when you tell your arms and legs to move. Other messages are **automatic**. These include the ones your body sends when you're faced with a fear.

When you are scared, a lot of things happen in your body. You might start sweating and shaking. Your breathing may get faster, too.

The adrenal **glands** are on your kidneys.

That's because your brain has sent a message to your adrenal glands. These small organs pump out a **hormone** called adrenaline, which starts the body's fear response.

ADRENALINE

Adrenaline moves quickly through blood. It tells the body to get ready for action. This makes your heart beat faster and your muscles **tense**.

You get a burst of energy and your body works harder than usual. Your senses become sharper, helping you see and hear things better.

FALSE ALARM

The nervous system acts like an alarm for your body. This alarm goes off when it senses danger.

Sometimes, the alarm goes off even if there is no real danger. A phobia is like this. It can make your body respond to something that can't really hurt you.

★ WICKED ★ WITCHES

Who wouldn't be afraid of an evil witch? Secrets and **spells** that can cause harm would scare anybody. But some people have a phobia that there are real witches who practice dark magic!

They will do anything to avoid those they think may cast a spell.

Hundreds of years ago, there were witch hunts. People thought witches were hidden among everyone else. Could people they knew secretly be evil?

One of the most famous witch hunts led to the Salem Witch Trials. In 1692, more than 150 people in Salem, Massachusetts, were accused of being witches. Sadly, a total of 20 of them were **executed**.

★ BEASTLY ★ BEARDS

Do you know someone with a beard? Some beards are long and tangled, while others are short and rough.

No matter the size, beards send some people into a cold sweat. To you, beards may appear harmless. But for people with a phobia of beards, they can seem very scary!

Since beards are so fuzzy, some people are afraid of what could be mixed in with the hairs. Could there be dirt or crumbs tangled inside?

Others are afraid because beards cover a person's face. It's scary that they don't know what a person looks like behind their beard. Are they hiding something under all that hair?

★ NASTY ★ KNEES

What comes to mind when you think of the beach? You may think about the nice, hot weather. Or you could imagine people wearing shorts and swimsuits. That's when the knees come out!

For some, seeing knees is a nightmare. Bony, wrinkly, hairy, or bruised, all types of knees give people with this phobia a bare legged scare.

For people with a knee phobia, just the thought of them causes panic. They might get scared of their knees touching someone else's. Some may not even like to see their own knees!

How could a fear of knees start? It might have begun with a knee injury from a while ago. When a person with this fear sees knees, they may remember getting hurt.

TEETH
★ OF ★
TERROR

Many people don't like going to the dentist. But for those with a phobia of dentists, it can be a nightmare!

People with this phobia may fear being trapped in the dentist's chair. Some might be afraid of the dentist poking their teeth and gums. What might they find inside?

When people are scared of going to the dentist, they may avoid getting their teeth checked for a long time. This can cause painful problems with their teeth.

Your teeth will start to **decay** if you don't keep them clean.

Although going to the dentist can be scary, it's important for our teeth. Visiting the dentist keeps them healthy and clean.

★ CANNOT ★ BARE IT!

Clothes keep us warm, especially during the winter. But do they also keep some people from facing a phobia?

Some people have a fear of being naked. Wearing no clothes makes them feel helpless and **exposed**.

This phobia can make everyday things harder to do. Showering may be difficult. So could changing clothes.

SCARED SPEECHLESS

Imagine speaking in front of a crowd with hundreds of people staring at you. All those blank faces are waiting for you to say something. Are you afraid?

A phobia of public speaking is common. It appears more often in younger people than in older people.

This fear is also called stage fright. It may cause sweaty palms and shaky knees when someone with this phobia steps in front of a crowd.

If you have a fear of public speaking, try practicing in front of your family and friends. This helps you feel more prepared and less afraid for the real thing.

★ EVIL ★ ITCHING

Do you feel that itch on your arm? It might be nothing . . . or it might be a bug!

Some people have a fear of bugs on their skin. It gives them the creeps! They might even get itchy at just the thought of it.

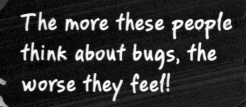

People with this phobia might scratch themselves a lot. They may also wash more often than usual to get rid of any bugs that may be hiding.

CREEPY CLOWNS

While clowns make things fun for some people, they might bring out fear in others. What is it about clowns that people find so scary?

Some people are afraid of how clowns look. With faces as white as skulls and noses as red as blood, they can give quite the scare.

Clowns have been around for thousands of years. Long ago, they were called jesters. These clowns would **advise** leaders and rulers. They would also make them laugh!

Today, a phobia of clowns is common. Those with this fear may be upset never knowing what clowns are going to do next.

Marilyn Monroe was a famous actor and model. She starred in 23 films, which earned her millions of dollars.

Marilyn had a difficult childhood. She also grew up with a phobia. . . .

Marilyn had a fear of speaking because she spoke with a stutter. Stuttering is when a person repeats the first sound of a word and finds it hard to say the rest.

To help with her phobia, Marilyn spoke slowly and carefully. This allowed her to say words without stuttering. She eventually became famous for her slow way of talking!

A PHOBIA ★ OF ★ PHOBIAS

That is the end of our circus of fears. Has anything scared you? Maybe what scared you the most is the feeling of being afraid.

Worrying about being scared is also a phobia. For some people, just the thought of fear is what frightens them!

Some people with a fear of phobias are scared of feeling the physical signs of fear, such as a tightness in their chest or sweaty palms.

If you've found out you have a phobia, don't worry. People with phobias can get help. Relax your body by breathing slowly or by practicing yoga. Talk to a trusted adult to learn more.

CURTAIN CLOSE

THANK YOU FOR COMING! WE HOPE YOU'VE ENJOYED EXPLORING DIFFERENT PHOBIAS. COME BACK SOON!

Stay brave until the next time you are forced to face your fears!

GLOSSARY

advise to help someone make a choice

automatic happening without being told to do something

decay to rot or break down

executed put to death

exposed made open to someone's view

glands parts of the body that help clean blood or release chemical signals

hormone a chemical made by certain glands in a person's body

nerves tiny body parts that carry messages to and from the brain

spells words believed to have magical powers

tense feeling nervous, often with tight muscles

INDEX

Read More

Colich, Abby. *Your Brain When You're Scared (Brainpower).* Minneapolis: Jump!, Inc., 2023.

Spalding, Maddie. *Understanding Phobias (Mental Health Guides).* San Diego: BrightPoint Press, 2022.

Learn More Online

1. Go to **www.factsurfer.com** or scan the QR code below.

2. Enter **"Human Phobias"** into the search box.

3. Click on the cover of this book to see a list of websites.